Dreams Matter
Unlocking the Treasures of Your Night

Geoerl W. Niles and Nancy Boyd

ISBN: 978-0-9881977-5-6

Printed in the United States of America

Dedication
And
Acknowledgments

I would like to honor several people for bringing this book into being.

First of all, thank you to my children and grandchildren who continue to inspire me to run the race with excellence and determination as they pursue their own dreams.

Second, thank you to the women who have taught me there is life after loss – Susan, Linda, Carol and Lynn.

Third, thank you Geoerl for birthing the dream of our book.

Fourth, I must thank and acknowledge Brent Lokker who has been the contextual editor on both of my writing projects. Brent, your keen insight and thoughtful suggestions have been invaluable.

Finally, I thank God for the dreams he's placed in my heart.

Nancy Boyd

This book is dedicated to my wife, Julianne who has never had a dream she could not describe in vivid detail. It was because of her I began asking God to help me remember more details in my dreams. You stand by me in all I do, you are an amazing partner, and a great dreamer like me. To my children and grandchildren, the ones I have now and those yet to come. When I was young I could not have imagined the amazing heritage that I would have, so I dedicate this book to you as well. My prayer is that you will always pay attention to your dreams and continue to move deeper into the revelation of who God is. His love for you is infinite, as are His mysteries… Dig deep, the treasure is great!

Geoerl W. Niles

Endorsements

God is a talking God. He often reaches out to us through our dreams to communicate things that will help us live the abundant life that He promised us (John 10:10). Yet many people do not understand their dreams, even when they are powerfully impacted by them. The Bible teaches that in the last days, when God pours out His Spirit on all flesh, "old men will dream dreams, and young men will have visions" (Joel 2:17; Acts. 2:28). We can expect that dreams will be an increasing phenomenon in the days to come. Therefore, it is important to have insight into this vital form of spiritual communication. If you are a dreamer – and you are aware that at times God Himself is talking to you – you need this book to guide you on the path of understanding so that you can have confidence in what God is saying because . . . your Dreams Matter!

Stacey Campbell
Shiloh Global

There are many ways God speaks, one of the ways is through our dreams. Do my dreams matter? Yes, they do.

God wants to speak to you and give you His truth. Dreams

can come from different sources so it's important to recognize the voice that's speaking. Throughout the Bible we see God speaking through dreams. I pray this book inspires you to research the Word to uncover how God has spoken through dreams to change the course of history.

My desire for you as you read Dreams Matter is that you would start dreaming about the will of God for your life and begin keeping a dream journal giving you the ability to record the happenings of your night as you wake.

Chris Overstreet
Compassion to Action

After growing up in church for most of my life, I remember sitting in my first guided prayer counseling session, called a "sozo", and the person had me ask God a question "Father is there a lie that I am believing about you?" Immediately in my head I heard Him respond "You think I am boring". I sat there aghast, almost horrified at myself, thinking "where did that come from? How could I think such a thing? God, do I really think You are boring?" Pondering this response which I didn't know was inside of me, I realized that if I was to be 100% honest, I did think my Father in Heaven was boring. You see I'd grown up in church my whole life and pretty much knew what the "right answers" were about God and situations. I had dumbed down my relationship with Him, to a series of right and wrong answers and because of this, my walk with Him was stale and dry as a bone.

So in that little room, I repented of that lie "God I'm sorry for thinking you're boring, please forgive me." I then said in expectation "What is the truth? What are you really like?" Immediately I saw a huge galaxy, immense and unlimited, sparkling in manifold color and beauty. Then I heard my Father say "Dave, I'm this big! Why don't you jump in and find out!". From that moment, God has stepped out of meetings, systems and religion and into my everyday life. I have been swept up into a dance with my creator, a true relationship with the unlimited one and he began to speak to me, my wife and kids through our dreams. Over these last eleven years, God has led us as and the movement we lead through paying attention to our dreams in the night. Even during critical moments, when we were unsure of what to do, God stepped into our night time and gave us blueprints needed to move forward successfully. My family and I now know that God is not a tame pussy cat, but He is unlimited and moving in our night times.

Dreams matter is an invitation for every one of us to discover the power of listening to God in our dreams. In this book you will be inspired to awaken your relationship with God and realize that He is speaking to you more often than you think. Right now, He is wooing all of us back to an intimate relationship with Him and it's not boring. This book will give you faith that God is talking to you; it will inspire you to take note and uncover His forward moving voice in something which you will probably spend 20 yrs of your life doing. Yes your dreams matter, get ready! Your Father in heaven can't wait to talk to you.

Dave Harvey
Co-Director Bethel Leaders Network

Geoerl Niles and Nancy Boyd provide an engaging one, two punch as they share from their own dream encounters how God uses our time of sleep to commune with our hearts and reveal greater insights than we might imagine. And for you who may struggle with disturbing dreams, they've offered invaluable wisdom to help you to continually navigate back to the goodness of God. In the spirit realm, there are not a lot of hard and fast rules, but rather a meandering journey of opportunities presented, including dreams, to engage you in drawing closer to the Lover of your soul. Upon reading Dreams Matter, I believe your spirit will be primed to be acutely aware of your heavenly Father's intentions to speak to you in the night season. Sweet dreams!

Brent Lokker
Author of Always Loved: You are God's Treasure, not His Project

Contents

Foreword

Don't waste your dreams.

That was the thought which I was left with after reading the manuscript of this book.

This is a book personally written with the kind of humility which draws the reader in. It says from start to finish that this is attainable for us all. Although it is practical, it is a guide into the supernatural, the unseen. I particularly liked this description of a dream: "So God takes the opportunity to speak to my spirit while my logic is asleep."

This beautiful articulation of perhaps what the Psalmist was implying: "He instructs my mind in the night season," Psalm 16:7 is a great invitation to take note of the instruction and insight contained in this guide to dreams.

In particular this call to take our nights seriously is worthy of note: "Dreams are things that should make us feel happy or at the very least inquisitive when we wake up. It's my opinion that even the crazy dreams should cause us to be a little excited to discover what God is telling us. So why is it then,

2

that so many are waking up more exhausted than when they went to sleep? It's actually quite simple, we have taken our nights for granted. Instead of preparing for our rejuvenation, we simply lay down and close our eyes, hoping to get a good night's rest."

But taking back our nights we learn is not only for us but for a greater purpose: "Taking back our nights is essential to revival, and to personal victory in our lives. Oh... and it's also the way back to a peaceful night sleep."

Also of great value is the explanation of the dream filter, which we all have. Understanding this will hopefully lead us to: "Like Joseph we need to believe in our ability to sniff out the meanings of our dreams and know that God is for us not against us, so we will be blessed by our dreams correctly viewing them through God's voice,"

This final advice from the book is excellent:

"Process your dreams. Process them with God, with trusted friends who know you and with anointed counselors. If you process your dreams, you will find the voice of God is increased to you because he is speaking in your waking and in your sleeping."

Well done Geoerl and Nancy. This is a little gem, packed with nuggets, carrying an invitation and increasing hunger to understand our nocturnal narrative.

Paul Manwaring
Author of Kisses From a Good Father and
What On Earth Is Glory?

Preface

I woke up this morning looking out a window that displayed the immense beauty of the Oregon Coastline. Yesterday Julianne, my wife, and I arrived here for a quick refresh and renewal. As we walked on the beach, I silently marveled at how God created such an amazingly peaceful scene by speaking into existence one of the most violent forces of nature. The ocean can be dangerous, lonely, violent, and brutal, yet there is nowhere else that I can find peace like on the shoreline of the Oregon coast. Now you can argue that there are more pristine or beautiful places in the world, and you would most likely be right, but the coastline here has such violent beauty, I don't think there is anything else quite like it for me.

This book may not look like the kind of book about dreams that you are used to seeing. It is a book that will encourage you to pay attention to your dreams. Like the ocean in front of me, your dreams can seem brutal and dangerous, but if you train yourself to look at them through God's perspective, you may find keys to unlock potential. They might just become the unparalleled source of peace in your life they were meant to be, and let's face it, we all need our nights to be a place of peace, not a place of unrest. The enemy has tried to steal our nights, and it's time we took them back! I believe that our dream life is paramount to understanding the call on our lives and that through proper insight and perspective, you will find your dreams to be like a great big treasure hunt every morning searching for gold in our dreams.

Bill Johnson, Pastor of Bethel Church in Redding, California, once said our nights are not the end of our day but the beginning of our day. If that is true, God must have intended to make our sleep powerful so our days would be ordered.

Dreams Matter was born out of a personal need to understand how God speaks to us.

He is not a boring God but finds creative ways to speak life into us. God wants our attention. We would discount revelations if they were simply thrown into our laps in a casual conversation from a friend or even through a sermon. While we gain many insights into ourselves through means like this, our dreams are very personal. By giving us secrets and revealing truths through our dreams, God allows us to hear in a less guarded place. My hope is through this book, you will start to look at your dreams with an expectation of receiving revelation and new tools for life. You will learn to not dismiss your dreams out of hand as chaotic thought but actually recognize it as a way God communicates.

Chapter 1
Tools That Are There When You Need Them
Geoerl

I felt the sand beneath my feet as I ran towards the only building in sight. I felt the need to get away from this place, and this structure seemed to be the only way out. As I reached this rundown shack, I noticed that there was some sort of transportation just to the left of the porch; I knew this was my answer but how did it work? The machine in front of me reminded me of a motorcycle, but so much more. I knew that if I could get this thing started, it would very likely be able to carry not only myself but anyone who wanted to go with me. It would not start. Obviously, the machine had been sitting for quite some time as evidenced by the rust and cobwebs. I knew what I needed to get it started, but I found myself without the tools I needed to complete the fix. Then out of nowhere, I thought to myself, I was given this tool a long time ago, and for some reason, I wasn't carrying it with me. I remember actually saying out loud... "I need to go back to that moment where I received that tool and bury it right over there in the sand."

It seemed so obvious that all I needed to do was to go over and dig in that spot, and I would find the tool I needed to fix the transport, simply because I went back and buried it there for this moment in the future. I woke up thinking, wow, that was a crazy dream. I wonder what it means and does it really matter. Right then, I began a journey that has led me to write this book. A book that honestly asks the question... Do my dreams matter?

It was not long after this dream that I read a Facebook post from a friend of mine asking a question. Does anyone know a good resource for dream interpretation? I immediately heard the Holy Spirit say, "Yes, the one that you two will write!"

"Yes, the one that you two will write!"

I started to laugh out loud, and as I'm writing about this, I'm glad that God did not do what he did with Sarah when she laughed at the angel who said she would bear a child in her old age. Instead, he just smiled and said, "You heard me."

It was such a direct, clear word that I messaged my friend and said, "You may think I'm crazy, but I heard the Lord say that you and I will write the book that helps people find meaning in their dreams." She reacted pretty much the same as I did and said it would have to be a God thing because she felt she didn't have the expertise to write on that subject. Yet, she agreed that we should pray and explore this.

Changing an old way of thinking is not as simple as just choosing to think differently...

About a month later, I revisited this dream, and I asked God what does this mean? I started to think about the pieces, and slowly the picture began to form in my mind. I needed to escape the place that was falling apart, not because I was in danger but because it was an old way of thinking or an old mindset. In other words, I was trying to put a new revelation from Holy Spirit into an old wineskin. In ancient times, winemakers found that if you put new wine into an old used wineskin, it would crack and burst, spilling the new good wine out and wasting it. So as I realized God was teaching me a new truth, I needed to get out of my old way of thinking, or I would simply crack, and the fresh revelation would be spilled out and wasted.

The vehicle looked at first glance like it was made for just me, but as I looked closely, I realized it could hold many, many more. If I learned to move away from old thinking, I would be enabled to take people with me. Truth is like that, It draws a crowd. When Jesus started to teach, what began as one or two people grew into five thousand. Truth is contagious.

Changing an old way of thinking is not as simple as just choosing to think differently. It actually takes some tinkering. Sometimes your thoughts are so set, they become rusty and full of cobwebs. In many cases, it seems so hopeless you may just turn away and reject the revelation because to grab that truth requires too much work.

In this case, it not only would necessitate my willingness to clean up and dust off my thinking but also required a tool that I was not currently carrying with me. Instead of letting this frustrate me, I realized that God had given me everything I needed for this shift. All I needed to do was to draw that into the situation. In the dream, it manifested as my going back in time and burying that tool right next to where I would eventually put it to use. I simply needed to walk over to the spot and dig it up.

In reality, the tool is with me. The truth is this, I will receive tools in my life that seem out of place sometimes, but my response must not be to throw it away but to realize it may not be for this season. My Father would not give it to me if he didn't expect me to use it at some point. So I strategically put it in a place where I will be able to use it when the time comes.

As we continue forward, my hope is to be transparent as we walk out the truths that can be uncovered in our sleeping dreams. Too many of us have been frustrated by dreams that don't make sense. I am asking God to give us all the tools required to unlock the secret of our spiritual dreams. Remember, not every dream will be significant to our journey; let's face it, sometimes it's just bad pizza right before bed.

So, here's to the dreamers, Let's Go!!!!

Chapter 2
Pay Attention
Nancy

When there is no clear prophetic vision, people quickly wander
astray. But when you follow the revelation of the word,
heaven's bliss fills your soul.
Proverbs 29:18 TPT

When Geoerl messaged me that we were supposed to write a book on dream interpretation, I confess I had my doubts. After all, the only reason the subject came up was that I'd asked who was a good source for interpretation. And then one of my best friends in the world says it will be us. Hmmm. Since then, I've been pressing in to really seek God for the understanding of my own dreams, and it's been fascinating how he's been opening them up. Even minor dreams that I wouldn't usually pay attention to seem to contain some fairly significant meanings. So here goes.

Dreams. Most people have them or, should I say, remember having them. I know I have always dreamed, although I never really paid much attention to them unless they were super intense or super scary. Let's be honest, the scary ones stay with you for a while. However, in recent years I've begun to realize that dreams often contain words from God that I've been closed off to in my waking hours. These are messages that are often inconceivable to my logic or don't fit my preconceptions. So God takes the opportunity to speak to my spirit while my analytical nature is asleep. I once heard someone say that the closer you draw to God, the less you will dream because communication lines are stronger, and he doesn't need to speak through dreams. I don't know if I agree with that, but I do believe dreams are often the spirit realm's language.

Dream interpretation can be tricky and tenuous. Sometimes a dream is just a dream, and sometimes it can be a game-changer. Even the least significant dreams can be substantial. Two days before my husband was diagnosed with stage four pancreatic cancer, I had a dream. I don't remember any of the dream except for this one part. I was on my way to an unknown destination when a man I passed on my way said to me, "I'm so sorry about your friend." When he said this, I began to weep with deep sobs. That's it. I woke up and said a quick prayer like, "Lord, I pray all my friends are OK." Two days later, I found myself telling my kids about their dad's illness, and as I did, those same gut-wrenching sobs came over me. I flashed back to that dream and realized it had been a warning and a direction to pray that I'd ignored. It was inconceivable that the "friend" referred to in the dream was my soulmate and closest friend. If I'd taken the time to stop and seek God for the meaning of that dream, I might have responded sooner in prayer. As it was, I'd lost valuable time on my knees. (Some people mistakenly believe that dreams like that are precognitive of set events, but I think they're warnings crafted to encourage some action on our part.)

I want to encourage you to pay attention to your dreams, start recording them and keep an open heart and mind about interpreting them. Two of our favorite Old Testament heroes were dream interpreters - Daniel and Joseph. They had no official "training" in the field, only strong faith in the face of adversity and ears to hear. Let's explore the language of sleep imagery and see if we also have "ears to hear."

Chapter 3
Taking Back What The
Enemy Has Stolen
Geoerl

For God does speak—now one way, now another —
though no one perceives it.
In a dream, in a vision of the night, when deep sleep
falls on people as they slumber in their beds,
Job 33:14-15 NIV

Upsetting, unsettling, unnerving, disconcerting, disturbing, and troubling. These are words that I have heard used and even used myself to describe dreams. But what if? What if they could consistently be changed to terms like fulfilling, rewarding, gratifying, constructive, worthwhile, valuable, beneficial, and even exciting? It's not only possible but probable when you begin to understand the purpose of your dreams.

We use terms like ... "What are your hopes and dreams?" ... "He's just a dreamer" ... or ... "that's the stuff dreams are made of." All good things, all things that create a feeling of wellbeing. We even write songs about dreams. "A dream is a wish your heart makes ..." or "dream a little dream with me."

Dreams are things that should make us feel happy, or at

the very least curious when we wake up. It's my opinion that even the crazy dreams should cause us to be a little excited to discover what God is telling us. So why is it then that so many people are waking up more exhausted than when they went to sleep? It's actually quite simple, we have taken our nights for granted. Instead of preparing for our rejuvenation, we simply lay down and close our eyes, hoping to get a good night's rest.

> ***We must be aware of the fact there is a spiritual battle for our attention.***

We read in reports mattresses were an 18 billion dollar per year industry in 2018. It is projected that by the year 2023, it will add an additional billion dollars in sales! Wow, that is incredible considering that just 30 years ago, it was crazy to think of buying a new mattress before you got every ounce of life out of your old one! The question is - why? I believe it's because we have allowed our nights to be invaded by an enemy who wants to steal, kill, and destroy. As a population, we are looking for a physical solution to a spiritual issue. We take sleep aids, use "essential" oils, buy pillows that are supposed to help us breathe better and mattresses that will magically enable us to wake up refreshed. As ones that are "called according to his purpose," we must be aware that there is a spiritual battle for our attention.

We don't want to give place to our nightmares or even dreams that make us feel unsettled. But if we have the correct outlook, and we are consistently giving our nights over to Holy Spirit to promote and educate us, we will see that even in dreams we would consider bad, there are things that we can glean from them. Romans 8:28 says, "And we know that God causes all things to work together for the good of those who love God and are called according to his purpose..."

All things!! Not just the obvious stuff but the things that are confusing or frustrating!!

We want it to be easy, but sometimes it just isn't! Can I say that out loud? Is it alright for a leader to tell you that not everything is easy? There are times where we must seek the treasure that God has laid out for us. I say it's worth it... It's worth the effort to seek to find the good God has set before you.

If you take what is in this book seriously, I believe that the voice you hear in your dreams will be from God, not our enemy. And even when we find ourselves in weak moments and the enemy slips in an attack, you will recognize it for what it is, throw it away, and get right back on track. Let those moments serve as a reminder to ask Holy Spirit to utilize your nights and not give the devil a place to operate.

Chapter 4
What Filter Are You Using?
Nancy

I have had dreams, and I've had nightmares.
I overcame the nightmares
because of my dreams."
– Jonas Salk

I've dreamed all of my life. I never really thought a lot about them because it was so natural; they did not seem significant in any way. About a year after I surrendered my life to Jesus, I had a blockbuster dream that did not fade with the morning light. I'll save telling that dream for another chapter, but soon after, I realized that dreams were spiritual in nature. Why? Because every dream I dreamed began to be filled with demons who would pin me down where I couldn't move. I discovered quite by accident that if I could breathe out the name of Jesus, the paralysis would be broken.

This may sound like a challenge to some of you, but it was terrifying for me. I was in a mainline church that taught me how to be a better person, not how to fight demons in my dreams. I began to dread dreaming and would pray not to dream and plead the blood of Jesus over my mind so nothing could penetrate my thoughts as I slept. I found if I fell asleep without my "protection prayers," I would be demonically assaulted every time! Why was I so special? Why was the devil targeting me? Was I especially anointed as a threat to him? Actually no. Not any more than any other Christian walking in their identity and their legacy. By the way, I wasn't walking in either of those, but I was a pretty good person, and I passionately loved Jesus. I was also a functioning "fearaholic."

> *It was as if a light was switched on, and I began to attract the attention of the spirit realm..*

Allow me to interject why this is relevant. My friend, Ian Carroll, is an involuntary seer. That means he sees in the spirit realm even when he's not tuning into the spirit realm. Hence the term "involuntary." I've taken his seer course, and one of the things he teaches is that many children initially see demons and shut down their gift of seeing in the spirit. However, that's not the experience for all children. There are just as many children who see angelic beings. The difference is the filter we operate out of. If fear has found a place in our lives for some reason, we will tend to see fearful things. Similarly, if we feel safe and expect good things, we will tend to see the angelic.

When I "woke up" in the spirit and had my first encounter with God in a dream, it was as if a light was switched on, and I began to attract the attention of the spirit realm. Because fear was such a stronghold in my life, I drew every creature of fear around me. The more they showed up, the more I was afraid! Even after God set me free from fear, I would pray not to dream because I didn't realize my fear attracted those demons, not my faith!

However, once you know God speaks to us through our dreams, you don't really want to pray to NOT dream. I mean, who doesn't want to hear from God? So I changed my prayer. I pray that God will speak to me through my dreams and protect my dreams from being used by the devil. This has opened a whole new avenue of communication. My favorite conversations with God are the intimate ones in my early morning prayers and devotions. However, I've found he uses dreams to speak to me in a different way, and my filter is still super important.

For example, I come out of a very negative background where correction was always given with a critical tone, so I tend to filter my dreams through that experience. I often wake up from a dream feeling anxious or distraught because of how I interpret the meaning of what I've dreamt. I will remind myself that God isn't critical but encouraging and doesn't use shame or guilt to motivate. I will also remind myself that even though the dream felt "bad," it must have come from this good God because I had prayed for HIM to speak through my dreams, and he loves to interact with us. Once I retrain my brain, I invite him into the conversation and ask why I dreamt that dream and what he wants to say in it? Here's an example: I dreamt I was driving a car full speed ahead. I could see the freeway I wanted to be on ahead of me, but as I neared it, I hit a dead-end, so I turned left. Still full speed ahead, instead of coming to a side street, I hit another dead end. I woke up frustrated and upset.

"God, am I headed the wrong way? Have I missed your directions and taken my own way?" I didn't get much of a response, which only amplified my anxiety. I felt like God was chastising me. That he was saying, I had missed his plans and was careening forward to nowhere.

Once I settled down in my oversized black leather recliner with my coffee steaming, my sliding window fully open to let in the morning air, and my journal and Bible at hand, I went through the retraining of my brain. God loves me. He doesn't send dreams of failure out of the blue. I must stop analyzing this and let him address what this dream was about. This is what he said. "You feel like no matter how hard you work or how fast you go, you are getting nowhere fast. I want you to trust me with your detours. I am leading you to the place I want you to be, even if it seems like nothing is happening. Trust me with your roadblocks and detours."

He doesn't send dreams of failure
out of the blue ...

BAM! What a difference from my original interpretation where I'd assumed God was showing me I was headed away from his plans. That I'd disqualified myself in some way. He wasn't correcting me but revealing my own frustrations and his faithfulness in the midst of them. I hadn't realized how frustrated and discouraged I'd become by some closed doors, but he did. He showed me what I felt was happening and then enabled me to identify it. He articulated for me what I could not say for myself, and then he brought comfort and hope. So good.

Consider the filter you use when you interpret your

dreams. Have you invited God to speak through them? Believe he will. Have you asked him to protect them? Again, believe he will. Consider the fruit of your interpretation - how does it make you feel? God doesn't need shame, guilt, or condemnation to motivate you. Does it line up with his written word? He is not contradictory. Finally, would Jesus say it? Filter your understanding through the truth of this: God is good, God loves you, and God is for you.

Chapter 5
So Why Dreams?
Geoerl

> The future belongs to those who believe in
> the beauty of their dreams."
>
> – Eleanor Roosevelt

We are a people who tend to fill our days with things. Even though many of those "things" would be considered good, they are still, at times, filler to our days. It is at the core of my beliefs that God is speaking to us in every moment of every day. Most of the time, we cannot hear him over the filler. That's where I believe dreams come in.

While you are dreaming, you are more open to how God speaks. In those moments, we start to feel maybe a little overwhelmed by the imagery that God uses to gain our attention. But when we begin to filter our dreams the way that Nancy speaks about in the previous chapter, we begin to understand our Father's voice a bit better.

Science would tell us that dreams are the mind's way of working through unresolved emotional issues and conflicts. Dreams are simply a process to better deal with our circumstances. While I agree there is truth in these thoughts, I believe dreams were meant for more.

How many times has our enemy taken a situation where God calls us champions and caused us to feel completely defeated?

In Genesis, the story of Joseph is one of our first encounters with "Dreams that Matter" in the Bible. In his dreams, he was shown not only his brothers bowing down to him but also his parents. Joseph being young and a bit naive, was so enthusiastic about the dream. He didn't stop to think about the repercussions of telling the dreams to his family. In retrospect, as readers of the story, we can look at the whole event and see a plan in motion. This plan would eventually be essential to the survival of his family and even the entire Jewish population. Still, at the time, it looked like the dream would cause him to suffer greatly, even die. Joseph would find people do not always understand the significance of a dream the way the dreamer does. Dreams can cause others in your life to doubt your calling or even your ability to hear clearly from the Lord. It is, therefore, critical to seek holy council when determining meanings in dreams and visions. In

Joseph's zeal to walk out the calling God had given him as a leader, or maybe even a ruler, he forgot to think about the way his older brothers would react. He did not consider that his brothers would feel that he was acting superior or taking the talents they possessed and their status as older brothers for granted. The betrayal they felt resulted in a plot to kill him. If not for his brother Judah's intervention, they would have slit his throat and told his father wild animals had devoured him and carried him off, rather than selling him off as a slave. Joseph, believing he was meant for greatness, was now in the back of a wagon shackled and bound, meant for nothing more than servitude. How many times has our enemy taken a situation where God calls us champions and caused us to feel completely defeated? If he can cause us to lose our vision, even for a moment, he can cause confusion that may take us years to unravel.

Our dreams might cause us to become uncomfortable or even frightened. Instead of looking for the cause or value in our dream, we may let it paralyze us. If we could see the end result, as we do in Joseph's story, even disturbing dreams would enable us to trust His ability to speak and guide us even through dreams that cause distress. There will be dreams that have no intrinsic value to us. Having attuned our hearing to His voice, we will recognize them for what they are and quickly and simply dismiss them.

Joseph had a real situation where he felt like he understood the meaning of the sheaves of wheat bowing to him. Only to have his reality say no, they won't bow, they will attempt to kill you! At this moment, he could have stopped believing that he had the ability to understand dreams. Instead, he continued to believe in his ability to hear God well and interpret the cupbearer and the baker's dreams. As Joseph walked out the story God had crafted for his life, he saw nations saved in a time of great depression and famine. Joseph was relegated by man to a prisoner's status but elevated to the position of ruler by God. In the end, what God was showing Joseph in his original dream was this: he was to become a ruler but it would be in Egypt. Joseph now had the power to control the food reserves in a time of famine, and his brothers were forced to come to Egypt and ask for the food they needed to survive the seven years of famine that was now afflicting the land.

This story has many facets that are essential to understanding our ability to listen well, even in times of self-doubt. I encourage you to take the time to read it for yourself and be inspired. It can be found in the first book of The Bible, Genesis chapters 37-47.

Like Joseph, we need to believe in our ability to sniff out the meaning of our dreams and know that God is for us, not against us. Then we will be blessed by our dreams correctly, viewing them through God's voice. Still, first, we must give over our nights to the Holy Spirit and not let the enemy steal our sleep.

Bill Johnson from Redding California's Bethel Church has said, your night is actually the beginning of your day. In other words, your day does not begin when the alarm goes off at 7:00AM but when you close your eyes the night before. Therefore, it is essential to start your sleep with a prayer that would say something along these lines: "Holy Spirit, I give my night to you, and I ask that you would speak to me during the night and let me come into a deeper relationship with you through my dreams."

Suppose we continue to treat our time of rest as just a chance to go into a vegetative state of sleep. In that case, we will continue to miss the most valuable time for our Father to speak to us and into us. Learning this key will cause you to stop going to bed without first asking God to utilize your time of rest to promote your level of relationship with Him. Now I'm not saying that I've never fallen asleep from exhaustion and not said those words, but once it was in my spirit, I knew I was covered.

Chapter 6
A Rose is a Rose Unless It's a Cat
Nancy

As for me, Daniel, my spirit within me was anxious, and the visions of my head alarmed me. I approached one of those who stood there and asked him the truth concerning all this.

Daniel 7 15-16b ESV

I love prophetic symbolism! I love how vehicles often represent ministry models, and babies represent new ministry or the birth of a long-awaited opportunity. I love to think that when my husband or my mom shows up in a dream, they are more than likely a type for the Holy Spirit or an angel. Recognizing a common understanding of symbolism often gives me a starting place to understand what God is saying to me in my dreams.

However, there is a danger in applying symbolic meaning across the board. I don't think God ever intended for us to rely on a dream dictionary over his voice, and our dreams are usually very personally directed. I'm not saying that these tools aren't valuable - they are - but we have to start with what the things in our dreams represent to us personally, how we felt in the dream, what our current circumstances are. Let me give you an example.

During my husband's battle with cancer, I had a dream that a white, fluffy cat had come into our hotel room through a vent. The cat was very affectionate, rubbing against my legs and jumping into my lap. Instead of enjoying this, I became worried in the dream. I found that its fur began to seriously hinder my breathing, and I woke up feeling somewhat panicked. I asked for help with interpretation and found many people responded that cats represented love and comfort. If not for my sense of distress, I could have said yes, that's what that cat was trying to do.

...*not all comfort and comforters are safe.*

I continued to be troubled for a few weeks because I knew the dream was significant, but I didn't know what God was trying to say. That is until I ran into a woman I hadn't seen in quite a while. As we began to chat and catch up, I shared what was going on with Bert and our hopes for divine healing. Her response was meant to comfort, but I realized that as she kept repeating "Poor, poor you," this was not comfort or support but toxic pity. The more I affirmed we were hopeful, the more she reiterated, "Poor, poor you." The longer I stood there trying to convince her our situation was not hopeless, the more I could feel the temptation to buy into that pity. I finally ended our conversation with some remark about God still heals today and escaped. As I walked away, I flashed on the cat that had suffocated me, and I heard the Holy Spirit say, "Remember your dream? I was warning you that not all comfort and comforters are safe." Click. I got it.

A couple of months ago, I had another dream about cats. In this dream, my cat Sassy was with me. Sassy died a couple of years ago after living a long life of nearly 20 years as our cat. Also in the dream, was my cat Cookies, whom I hadn't seen in over a month. (All of our cats are outside cats.) She just appeared to Sassy and me, and I was so surprised I said, "Cookies! Where have you been?" (I had assumed that Cookies had passed away and gone to kitty heaven too.) Following Cookies' appearance was a new kitten that was clearly meant to be part of our "family."

Before I go any further, I should confess I am not a pet parent or a fur mama. As you probably noted, I didn't know if my cat was alive or dead. I quit putting food out for her when she stopped showing up to eat it. I wasn't grieved at her passing any more than I had been at Sassy's. I certainly did not want a new cat, which only represented another responsibility to me.

Waking from the dream, I went into a conversation with God, "What was that about? I don't want any more cats!"

He began to reveal how some things in my journey were foundational, and I would always have them. Sassy was like that - the older cat, the constant for so long. Then he said some things that I thought were lost were being returned - Cookies. (She actually came home shortly after that dream.) Hearing him was so encouraging because I'd just come through a terrible season of loss. Then he said, "Not only am I restoring what you think is lost, but I'm increasing your metron (area of influence) with brand new things - the kitten." Now I'm assured, encouraged, and excited because of three cats in a dream!

In summation, there are many things to take into account in the language of dreams. Questions like "How did it make me feel?" and "What does [insert symbol] mean to me personally?" We can even ask, "Is this dream for me or someone I know or a nation or something else?" Is the dream meant to stir you to action, a warning, or information?

Ultimately, we have to ask God what he's saying before we look to anyone else for interpretation because he is actually trying to communicate something when he speaks into our dreams. He's not trying to be mysterious or cryptic or obscure. He uses our dreams to graphically express what he wants us to know through pictures and a storyline. There are many resources to help you interpret your dream, but I urge you to start with the author first.

Chapter 7
Dreams That Cause Vision
Geoerl

He had a dream in which he saw a stairway resting on the earth, with its top reaching to heaven, and the angels of God were ascending and descending on it. 13 There above it[c] stood the Lord, and he said: "I am the Lord, the God of your father Abraham and the God of Isaac. I will give you and your descendants the land on which you are lying.

Genesis 28:12-13 NIV

Some dreams are so intense that they become impossible to stop thinking about. I'm talking about dreams that bring vision or clarity to vision. These dreams can be as simple as a keyword in a dream that sticks with you long after you wake, to whole storylines that have multiple parts needing to be explored.

I remember a dream where I was sitting on stage in a church I had visited only a couple of times for conferences. In the dream, I was playing a board game. Several others were playing as well. The stage had been stripped down, empty of everything except folding chairs and folding tables. After a few minutes, someone came and said it was time to set the stage for worship, and we would need to pack up and leave the area. As I picked up the pieces and headed towards my car, I realized one of the tiles from the game was missing. Usually, this would be no big deal, you see, I have seven kids, and games are rarely without missing pieces mere hours after opening. In this case, I felt a sort of panic, thinking I was missing that piece. In the dream, I went back inside and asked to look on the stage to see if I could find the missing tile. A janitor started helping me who had been pushing one of those over-sized dust brooms across the stage. Looking back, I'm pretty sure he was not merely a janitor. We looked on the stage and in garbage cans and eventually went behind the stage to look in the back rooms where he thought it possibly could have ended up. As we walked down the hallway, we walked through a door inside; there was a large commercial type kitchen, I thought it was strange in a church. We then went to the boiler room for some reason and searched to no avail. I left the dream knowing I had somehow lost a pivotal piece to the game, and I also realized at that moment, it was the tile that had the letter E.

I knew I needed this piece to understand my calling…

This dream became so important to me that I told all of my trusted friends about it to see what they thought it might mean. I wrote about it, I talked about it, I daydreamed about it. I knew I needed this piece to understand my calling - now - as well as what would be coming in the future. Incredibly within about a year or less, I was back for a conference. As we lined up for prayer, I realized that the line to enter the healing rooms this year was much longer. Rather than a straight line down the side hall into the overflow room, the line went down a hallway on the opposite side of the facility and wrapped around the entire sanctuary. As I walked down the second hallway that would have been directly behind the stage, it began to look familiar. I knew I had never been down this hall because every other time I had visited, it had been blocked off for staff only. As I stood there with my friends, I realized that this was the back hallway in my dream! Remembering the details of the dream, I told my wife and friends what was happening. Gathering my courage, I pointed and said, "If I walk down the hall to that door and there is a commercial kitchen behind it, I'm gonna be blown away."

Guess what was behind that door? A commercial kitchen! The details in my dream were exact. I had never been in that part of the church before, but my dream had made it real. This put a punctuation mark on the importance of the dream.

Here I sit some eight years later, and only portions of this dream have been clarified. There are obvious pieces that made sense right away, but others yet to be revealed. I know that in time, the Lord will unveil the answers exactly when I am ready.

This dream has been something that I go back to when making significant decisions in my life. I look at many situations and ask, "Is this the missing piece?" Or "Father, am I missing something as I move forward?"

It has become part of my vision casting for new ventures or new possibilities. While I don't always go back to this dream for every decision, I have asked God to bring it forward in my mind if there might be a connection.

Dreams can be simple and straight to the point, or as in this case, they can take years to work out. Our Father has placed treasure throughout our life. We should be ready to have our boundaries expanded for His truth to be revealed.

Chapter 8
It's All About Me, Je-e-esus
Nancy

When I was still very young in my relationship with the
Holy Spirit, I accompanied a friend to a Women's Aglow
meeting. As a United Methodist, this charismatic experience
was way out of my wheelhouse. The speaker for the day was
passionate and inspirational and offered to pray with anyone
who needed prayer.

At the time, I was deeply troubled by my oldest son's choices
and apparent distance from Jesus. I wanted to share my
situation with this wise woman and ask her to pray for my son
to turn to God. After I explained my heart, she looked me
straight in the eye and said forcefully, "The anointing isn't just
for you." Then she turned to the next person waiting to speak
to her. (The offer to "pray for people" had actually been an
invitation to receive prophecy. Not coming out of a
charismatic tradition, I didn't realize what was meant.)

Wait ... what?! What the bleep is "the anointing?" and
what did it have to do with my prodigal son? I'd only been a
believer for about a year and a half in a mainline evangelical
church, and I'd never heard of "the anointing." I didn't realize

she had not responded to my question but instead responded to what she sensed God intended for my life. Unfortunately, I didn't have the maturity or experience with the prophetic to process what had just happened. I felt like I'd been reprimanded. I walked away from the encounter, stunned by what seemed to be a rebuke to a request for prayer. It was years before I understood what had happened. She was seeing me through a prophetic lens. I doubt that she actually heard my request. She was so intent on speaking what she heard from God. She saw an anointing and call upon me and prophesied I was called to impart those things to others and not keep them to myself. What she had given me was actually a gift for the future. Those words have inspired me to equip and empower anyone willing to learn throughout my ministerial career. Still, her delivery left a lot to be desired, and I learned from that too.

Why am I sharing this story? Frankly, because I want you to hear what I'm about to say softly, not as a rebuke but as an encouragement. Ready? Your dream life is not just about you. As you begin to really tune into what you are hearing through your dreams, you will discover he is not only revealing things for you to know, but things meant for others. Not everyone is prepared to hear him, waking or sleeping. But if we are willing, sometimes through our dreams, he will reveal mysteries for our ears only. Other times he will reveal mysteries to be shared with others.

An example of this is revealed through a dear friend who is an apostolic intercessor to nations. She receives prophetic dreams that are about the times we are in or the times that are coming. Her dreams are quite complex and lengthy (and rarely a quick read), but I am often amazed at how accurate they are in retrospect. She will write out each dream in detail, and upon completion, she will ask God for the interpretation. Does she receive dreams that are for her personally? Yes, and she keeps those to herself. But she's worked hard discerning the difference and has encouraged many people with the dreams God has given her to share.

I must confess most of my dreams are all about me, me, me. Every once in a while, I'll get a word to be shared, but more often than not, God is still working on me. I'm not ashamed of that because it means he hasn't given up on me! When I receive a dream directed to someone else, I usually share the interpretation but not the actual dream. I don't want the symbolism in my dream to confuse or trip up anyone. I just share the bottom line and let whoever it's for hear the word, not the jumble of images used to deliver it. Sometimes God wants us to share the dream's detail, but I don't find that to be the norm for me.

Understanding our dreams comes through processing with God and draws us closer to God, but it must include the question - "who is this message for Lord, and how do I deliver it?"

Chapter 9
Equipped to Share ... Crossing the
Chicken Line
Geoerl

At Gibeon the Lord appeared to Solomon during
the night in a dream, and God said,
"Ask for whatever you want me to give you"

1 Kings 3:5 NIV

In the previous chapter, Nancy describes a time when she
needed a clearer understanding of a word given to her. While
the word was harsh and abrupt, she purposed to ask God if a
revelation needed to be received. After a time, she understood
God to be saying this, he gives us gifts for our own personal
benefit and equips us for ministry through those same gifts. In
this instance, the woman who gave the word was not hearing
a question or a prayer request but sensing a more profound
issue formative to Nancy's future ministry. I agree with my
friend that there was much left to desire in the way it was
delivered. My prayer is that we can have a gentler delivery
system when we get to reveal truth to others.

As with any of the gifts of the spirit, we find edification
in the gift of interpretation itself but often forget to look at the

50

gift through the lens of ministry to others. Experienced leaders find this simpler to exercise because they have collected ministry tools to guide them to promote others to a new level of understanding. It is more difficult for the novice to step across the chicken line and give a word of revelation to someone, especially if that person is a stranger.

> *... even the most outgoing people find it hard to put themselves out there and speak on God's behalf ...*

I remember a time, early in my ministry, when we had read the book "Treasure Hunt" by Kevin Dedmon. In this book, the reader was encouraged to ask Holy Spirit for clues about individuals that he wanted to give a word of encouragement to. For example, if Holy Spirit said to look for a person wearing a blue scarf and cowboy hat and was walking in the mall next to a baby stroller - I knew I should approach the person who fit that description and introduce myself. I should then say something along the lines of, "Hi, my name is Geoerl, and God has highlighted you to me." Then wait for Holy Spirit to encourage that person through me. In other words, get clues, go out, search for that person, and then uncover the treasure God sees in them.

Well, I decided I would go out on my own and try it. I prayed for clues, and the only thing that came to me was "Yellow Sweater," nothing else. So, I set off. I drove around my small town of Camas, Washington, searching for this "yellow sweater." I looked for at least an hour, amazed that not one person in this entire city was wearing a yellow sweater! I finally decided enough is enough. I said, "I guess I did something wrong..." I needed to go check the post office box for the church, so I made my way to the Post office, resolving to never waste my time again. I checked the mail and walked back out the Post office's front doors only to run, physically, into a woman wearing a pale-yellow sweater!!! It surprised me so much I just stared at her, and then... I walked right past her and drove away. I remember thinking... "I was expecting a bright yellow sweater, and that was a pale-yellow sweater, Wrong Person!"

Why am I telling you this? Because even the most outgoing people find it hard to put themselves out there and speak on God's behalf. I was eventually able to conquer that fear. Now I have experienced multiple life-changing exchanges when God showed up and really loved on people through myself and my family. Thanks, Kevin, for a fantastic tool to minister to people who need to know God sees them.

> ### *… we knew God was showing us both something significant.*

Your dreams can have a similar effect on people; here is an example. I was praying the other week about a dream that my wife and I experienced on subsequent nights. Our dreams were not exactly the same, but with so many similarities, we knew God was showing us both something significant. At a doctor's appointment, I shared how I was in the process of co-writing a book about the importance of dreams. My doctor friend was interested and asked, "OK, let me tell you about a reoccurring dream that I have, I know it means something, but I cannot figure it out!"

Because of my study on dreams and the truths that are being revealed by Holy Spirit as we write this book, I could pray at that moment and ask God to use me to bring this woman closer to Him. I shared what I felt God was telling her through this dream, and I believe she had a greater peace about it when I was finished. Dr. Doolittle (names have been changed to protect the innocent) is not a believer. I believe through that encounter with me that day, she will come to have questions about the reality of God and what that means in her life.

You see, "The anointing is not just for you" means this, he loves to bless you with all sorts of gifts and supernatural revelation. But just as much, he loves to partner with you to bless others. You were created to be sons and daughters of God, and in that, you have the privilege to see people touched by your Father through you!!! That is an incredible revelation in itself, and once we all cross that chicken line, the world will be a much brighter place.

Chapter 10
Why Are You Showing Me This?
Nancy

And having been warned in a dream not to go back to Herod, they returned to their country by another route.

Matthew 2:12 NIV

"I always know when someone is going to die."

That's what the young man (let's call him Joe) sitting across from me said as we sipped our Starbucks beverages. I'd met him at a networking luncheon for business people, and we'd arranged to get to know each other better. Joe was personable and bright and an atheist. I'd attended the luncheon at the invitation of a good friend. I must have appeared to be a promising lead to this young man who was an entrepreneur in the IT industry. Once establishing that I was not a good lead (as the pastor of a small church, my IT needs were pretty limited), we slipped into a casual conversation about ourselves.

"I always know when someone is going to die," Joe said with a smile. He was watching closely for my reaction. It was a little creepy. I half expected him to say something like, "you have three days to live."

"What do you mean?" I responded.

"I always have a dream before someone I know dies," he responded. He expounded on several instances of people close to him who died shortly after he dreamed they would.

Trying to avoid sounding religious, I shared with him how God gave some people a gift of a kind of foresight and that it was given for a purpose. I was trying to describe a prophetic sensitivity without using those exact words. He flat out rejected the thought. No, this extraordinary ability to predict death was because he was wired that way. He proceeded to describe a few other times he experienced foreknowledge in a dream - all unfortunate events. He didn't question if there were any purpose in his experience. It seemed he felt this ability was unique to him and set him apart. Although our conversation ended on a friendly note, we never connected again.

This wasn't the first time I'd heard of someone experiencing the prescience of the death of a loved one or friend. Usually, I would be told of God preparing someone for the passing of someone who had suffered an extended illness. "I knew mom would pass tonight." It was often the mercy of God to a loving family.

"Don't you think we should pray for the child not to die?"

However, one instance stands out in my mind. Sitting in a prayer meeting for pastors, one of my colleagues asked for prayer for a family member who he'd dreamed was about to lose their child. He didn't ask us to pray for the child to live, only that his family member be strengthened to face the loss. His dream had been so powerful, so real, he had no doubt the child would die.

As several of the people at the table agreed to pray, I felt compelled to interrupt. "Don't you think we should pray for the child not to die?" I asked.

My colleague was less than receptive to this train of thought. He knew this dream was from God, and he had no doubt that it would happen since it was God. I believed it was from God too, so I persevered.

"Sometimes God isn't revealing what is predestined but what is possible. I think he does it to motivate us to partner with him to pray against that possibility. In other words, I think you had that dream to prompt you to pray the child would be protected from death."

Although I could see he was unconvinced, several others around the table agreed we should pray for the child to be saved from harm. He relented to the wisdom of the majority. We prayed, and today, ten years later, his dream has not come to pass.

> *... dreams like this are not a prediction but a prompt to prayer*

Why would God reveal potential loss through a dream? Is it only to give us a secret knowledge of the future? Are we glimpsing a predetermined event? I can't answer that definitively since each dream is unique and specific to the dreamer. However, just like the child who did not die, I believe most dreams like this are not a prediction but a prompt to prayer. Sometimes he is trying to reveal the devil's designs, so we will pray and take a stand against him before he can bring about his plans for destruction.

Unlike my young atheist friend, I don't believe God reveals secret knowledge just for us to "know." My experience has been there's always a purpose. Whether it's to comfort and prepare you to release a loved one or move you to battle on someone's behalf, he does not waste his gifts. Ultimately, it comes back to asking him questions like "Why are you showing me this?" and "What do you want me to do with this?" Some may be skeptical because, if our prayers are productive, there is no death. They say it was just a bad dream. Perhaps. But I believe we saved a child's life in that prayer meeting. I also think many other tragedies never came to pass because I responded to my dreams as a warning, not a declaration. I guess there's no definite way of knowing this side of heaven, but I'm kind of looking forward to saying "I told you so" when I get there.

Chapter 11
A Call To Partner
Geoerl

He brought them to the man to see what he would name them; and whatever the man called each living creature, that was its name.

Genesis 2:19

Dreams are prevalent in the Bible. There are so many places where God uses our dreams to instruct, warn or give insight into a situation. God warns Laban not to interfere with Jacob and his plan to return to his own country. He gives insight into future events such as when we read the stories of Joseph interpreting Pharaoh's dream or Daniel interpreting the dreams of Nebuchadnezzar, and he instructs Joseph, Jesus' father, where to go to prevent Herod from finding Jesus as a baby. In each of these instances, he utilized dreams to accomplish His purpose, not only for the individuals but for the nation and the world.

I remember a dream/vision where I was escorted into the throne room of heaven. It was my first encounter where I remembered vivid details of God and the throne room surrounding him. The colors and the feeling of peace were beyond description. I could see a waterfall behind the throne that, to my amazement, flowed up instead of down. Later I would understand that this was the river of life that flowed from the Father, and as it flowed, it flowed from God into heaven and to the earth. Our understanding is so limited when it comes to the life that flows from God. As I stood there among the many, I looked and saw Jesus, and he caught my eyes with His and gave me a sideways head nod as if to say, "come with me." I followed him to my right and moved out of the throne room and into a side room where a doorway stood open. Even though I was with Jesus and standing in heaven, I felt turmoil as I looked into the darkness of the hallway in front of me.

"Jesus, go with me."

"If I were to go inside, I would not be able to show you what you need to see."

I began to walk, and as I entered the door, it seemed as if all light was gone. As if hearing my thoughts, I heard Jesus say: "Don't worry, I am always with you, and I will never leave you."

Which one will you choose?

I continued forward, and the hallway opened into a large room. I can only describe the feeling of it as something akin to a gymnasium or meeting hall. As my eyes adjusted, I began to see small candles, all lit, sitting on rows and rows of what seemed to be folding tables. In front of each candle, a person was sitting in a folding chair looking at the candle. It was clear they could not see anything beyond the light this small candle cast in front of them. My eyes focused on one woman somewhere in the middle of the hundreds of people in the room. As I watched her, she started to realize that there must be something beyond what she could see. She looked a bit sheepish and embarrassed, realizing that someone was watching her, but she could not see who it might be. Have you ever felt that feeling where you know people are watching you but could not see them? You want to look dignified even though you have no idea if they are really there or not? That is the look she had, trying to look normal but not quite achieving her goal, looking sheepish or embarrassed instead, constantly straighten her collar and brushing her hair back. I began to realize what Jesus was showing me was a picture of most of the world today. Everyone has some sort of understanding of the Light that Jesus brings into their life, but it is so limited they have no idea what it looks like beyond their little two-foot circle. As this realization was coming to me, I felt someone brush past me and walk to the row of tables where this lady was sitting. She turned into the row and walked right to the woman I had been watching. As she approached, she took the woman's shoulders, put her face right into the middle of this lady's candlelight, and smiled at her. The look of relief that came upon the first woman's face was palpable. I could feel her joy from across the room! I recognized the second lady as one of my team members from our church, and I felt pride that she was my friend. Kathy has since gone to be with Jesus, but what a light in my life she was. As I looked back to the scene, I saw Kathy get her out of her chair and begin walking with her toward the hallway where Jesus waited on the other side. I began to praise as I watched the scene unfold, and I heard Jesus simply say,

"Which one will you choose?"

Many people have such a limited understanding of what it means to live the words "Your kingdom come, your will be done, here as it is in heaven." They see only the little circle of light that matches their understanding, never thinking to ask for more revelation. It takes someone to walk into their situation and bring the light of Jesus with them. In my vision, Kathy represented the one who took the time to let someone know there was more than what they were aware of and then walk them to the light that would have lit up that entire room if he had walked through that hall with me. Jesus said that we are the light of the world, a city on a hill. he also told us to let that light shine. He could have walked into that room and revealed Himself to all of its inhabitants, but he chose to let us be the ones that show them the brightness of truth as we take them to Jesus. Now, I have seen and heard the testimony of times when Jesus has walked into someone's circumstances and snatched them from the hand of the deceiver. Also, I believe it has always been God's greatest joy to partner with his children. Just look at Adam in the garden; God told Adam to give the animals their names. As Adam gave the animals names, he was really speaking identity and character to them. We, like Adam, need to accept the privilege that he offers.

Through that dream, I realized the hunger inside of me. A hunger to see people saved and set free. Not only coming to the knowledge of Christ and what he has done to restore relationship, but also the "more" that God offers when we come into that relationship. I now feel a great responsibility to see people get out from behind the table where only a little light is revealed and walk through the door where the fullness of God is undeniable.

Chapter 12
The Process
Nancy

Long ago, at many times and in many ways, God spoke
to our fathers by the prophets, but in these last days he
has spoken to us by his Son, whom he appointed
the heir of all things, through whom also he created the world.

Hebrews 1:1-2 ESV

Much of what we've written has been to inspire you to pay attention to the way God uses your "nights" to speak to your spirit. As we have learned to value these messages from him, we want to encourage all believers to hear and see what the Lord is speaking to them and process the imagery and symbolism of their dream life. It is to the "process" that I'd like to say a final word.

Upon receiving a dream, I will often spend time with the Lord dialoguing. I will invite him to speak to me about it in intimacy. I often remind myself that he is not a God of fear, shame, or guilt and open myself to further revelation directly from him. This usually bears fruit because he sent the dream as a means of getting my attention.

However, some dreams must be processed in community. I'm not a fan of dumping my dreams out there for just anybody because I believe dreams are shaped uniquely to the person receiving the dream. However, we are called to be part of a "body." I mean to say that there is an aspect of accountability in sharing what you're hearing with trusted members of your faith community. When you are the sole source of your own enlightenment, the possibility of losing your balance increases. There is an increased wealth of knowledge in a collection of voices informed by God.

More importantly, your friend may have a critical perspective from their experience that you would have no way of knowing beforehand. For instance, I had a dream that included a picture of me cleaning up cement "pebbles" left behind by the construction of a cement house. The same night, one of the intercessors I work with dreamt I was climbing over rocks. On the face of it, I was not encouraged. Frankly, it sounded like more work and warfare to me. On the spur of the moment, I shared both dreams with a group of friends (one of whom was Geoerl) and asked what they thought. Immediately, Geoerl replied that God had reminded him of a time he and Julianne had ministered in the Dominican Republic. I won't give all the details here, but the bottom line is they helped a blind man over some rocks, and he began manifesting the tangible presence of heaven. He cried out, "I feel the rain of heaven!" and his head became drenched with no visible explanation. Geoerl's word to me was, "God is bringing you over rocks to step into a new level of the miraculous." Although I didn't describe the cement house from the dream to Geoerl, it was the same type of housing commonly found in the Dominican Republic. The fact that it was a blind man was significant because of the breakthroughs I've seen when praying for the blind. I would never have interpreted either dream in that way. My interpretation was "more work and warfare." Our meeting continued to be a dream "fest," with several of the other people involved sharing their dreams and receiving encouragement.

In another instance, I had an intense dream in which the Holy Spirit was driving me in a high-speed "muscle" car. We were going so fast I was looking for my seatbelt! Suddenly we stopped because there was a big, black chair with a white sign on it in the middle of the road. The Holy Spirit got out of the car and was staring at the chair intently. I kept saying just go around it (as many of the other vehicles were doing), but the spirit did not stop silently staring at the chair.

Eventually, I convinced him to go around it, and we went on. This was exciting because the vehicle was so powerful, and the Holy Spirit was speeding forward. Still, I was worried by the chair and being stopped. The only big, black chair I know is my quiet time chair, and I could not figure out how my quiet time would stop my forward momentum. Ugh! That dream was like having a seed stuck in your teeth and no toothpick. Finally, I talked to a man I know who has studied dream interpretation and asked what big, black chairs represent. He asked for further context, so I told him the dream. He responded that chairs often represent seats of authority. The fact that it was black and that the Holy Spirit had stopped to face it made him think it may be a stronghold or principality set against my ministry. Oh. Now I can see, God is warning me not to disregard or ignore resistance or roadblocks but to ask the Holy Spirit to help remove them. Quite different than my initial understanding that it must mean my quiet time was a hindrance.

Process your dreams. Process them with God, with trusted friends who know you, and with anointed counselors. If you process your dreams, you will find the voice of God is increased to you because he is speaking in your waking and in your sleeping.

Side note: Right after I began praying for help to remove the "black chair" roadblock, my black recliner broke. A bolt holding a spring in place broke in two very loudly one night. At first, I was devastated because I love that chair. Then I realized it was a prophetic sign that something had broken in the spiritual realm, and the stronghold blocking me had been disabled. Take your dreams seriously and, yes, I fixed the chair.

Chapter 13
An Invitation
Geoerl

…in fear and amazement, they asked one another, "Who is this?
He commands even the winds and water, and they obey Him."
Luke 8:25b NIV

Much of this book has been written in a non-threatening manner in order for you, the reader, to feel safe. Why? When God moves us into deeper revelation and relationship with Him, he doesn't just throw us in the deep end and hope we will swim. He teaches us how to thrive in our new surroundings. When I begin to stretch my capacity to understand the mysteries of God, He usually begins by gently nudging me toward wherever He wants me to go. For example, in 2008 I was happily filling the roles of music minister, youth pastor, drama pastor, and choir coordinator. A traveling evangelist, who also walked in the prophetic, was the guest speaker in our church one Sunday. After a fantastic worship service, this man began to minister prophetically. In the middle of speaking, God began to give him words of knowledge for people in the congregation. The words he gave were powerful, clearly the Spirit of the Lord was moving. Out of the blue, he looked in my direction and asked me to stand and bring my wife into the aisle. He began to unfold a word that God gave him about our calling and the fact that God would be moving us into a new position with greater authority. He quoted (Isaiah 54:2), *"Enlarge the place of your tent, stretch your tent curtains wide, do not hold back, lengthen your cords strengthen your stakes."*

It was a powerful word that I felt all the way down to my toes. My wife felt it too, as she began to tear up. I looked around and realized many in the church were beginning to murmur and give questioning looks to the speaker. He must have also noticed because it suddenly dawned on him who I was.

"Wait, you're the music pastor, aren't you?"

He immediately began to "walk back" the comments and explain that it didn't necessarily mean that we were leaving the church. He went on with the service a little embarrassed, trying to get back into the groove of his sermon. Julianne, my wife, and I sat there stunned by what was just spoken over us.

Now don't get me wrong. Following after the will of God in your life does not always feel safe. In fact, it's scary at times. God, on the other hand, is always safe. When we do what He's calling us to do, we can be sure in His ability to equip us. When the disciples were afraid of the storm that was threatening to sink their boat, they had likely lost sight of the fact that Jesus was the one who asked them to cross the lake in the first place. Jesus reacted in a way we may not expect... He gets up, asks the disciples where their faith was, and calms the storm that they are seeing. It is essential to understand this...Jesus doesn't come out of His place of rest to calm the storm; he actually calms the storm from his place of rest. He did not join them in their fear; he spoke to the wind and waves from his authority. (This story can be found in the book of Luke Chapter 8 vs. 22-25.) Jesus had been teaching his disciples how to act from a place of authority, and they had just missed an opportunity to practice what they had been learning.

When he asks them, "Where is your faith?" he's reminding them they are fully equipped to handle the storms themselves.

Over the next year, we revisited the word many times, unsure what to do with it. The economy was beginning to move into a recession, and the church's ability to pay our salary came into question. Although it was one of the most challenging times in our ministry, Julianne and I moved forward. The word God had given us helped navigate the adventure we would find ourselves on.

- **Enlarge the place of your tent...** Create space for a deeper understanding of the call on your life.

- **Stretch your tent curtains wide...** Open your eyes to the expanded territory that lays in front of you.

- **Do not hold back...** Don't rest on an old word but put everything you have into what God has laid before you. (run don't walk).

- **Lengthen your cords...** you are stepping out into a new revelation of who God is, don't worry about moving out from what has become "safe" in your world.

- **Strengthen your stakes...** Place your foundation firmly into the truth and the Word of God...It's gonna get wild!

So why am I telling you about a word of prophecy instead of a dream? This book is not meant to limit you to one way in which God speaks. Its actual purpose is to expand your ability to hear and see what God is saying and doing. Jesus was in Jerusalem and told the people... I do what I see the Father doing, (John 5:19), and I say what hear the Father saying. (John 12:49.) While you may get words from trusted friends or even strangers, you might also receive revelation through a gentle nudge from Holy Spirit. I believe dreams are one of the ways God gently nudges us toward our purpose. This book is about paying attention to the dreams we have at night, but you will find God speaks in visions, conversations with friends, and prophecy, among others. We believe you will find the strategies and tools found in Dreams Matter useful in these areas. The key is this... you must make sure your revelation always leads back to the Word of God. The word was given to us as a resource, a user's manual, if you will. All truth is found in the living Word of God, and nothing should be taken to heart without bringing it back to that word.

Our dreams carry verbal communication, but they also include visual communication. God has chosen to speak through dreams. It is our responsibility to pay attention. You may get a series of images that stir you to seek meaning or hear what the Father is saying while you sleep. Samuel, a prophet of God, was a young child when the Lord came to him while sleeping. Three times Samuel went to Eli, the priest thinking it was he calling him. Finally, on the fourth attempt, God came and stood next to Samuel and called his name. Samuel responded, "Here I am, Lord. Speak, for your servant is listening." (1 Samuel 3-10 NIV)

78

Nancy and I want to encourage you to use the tools at your disposal to correctly hear the word of God spoken through your dreams. Here are a few helpful ideas:

- Paul instructs us in Ephesians, don't go to sleep angry. "In your anger, do not sin, do not let the sun go down while you are still angry. Don't give the devil a foothold." Many of us need to remember restoration is key to rest. If you cannot restore right thinking before you sleep, the result may very well be "bad dreams." In this case, ask Jesus to help you forgive and bring your soul back to His peace.

- As stated earlier in this book, invite Holy Spirit into your night and into your sleep. God tells us that the fruit of Holy Spirit is love, joy, peace, patience, kindness, goodness, faithfulness, gentleness, and self-control. (Galatians 5:22-23) How many of us, if we could control our dreams, would ask for these life-giving fruits to be included? I believe nightmares would be a thing of the past if we would continually ask Holy Spirit to invade our dreams.

- Take note of dreams that are disturbing and not from God first thing in the morning. Think back to the previous day and find the place where your peace was taken and not restored.

- "Likewise, take note of mornings when you wake up, having had rest, and spiritual dreams revealed as you slept. Pay special attention to the things that were happening leading up to sleep.

- Journaling your dreams has proven effective in almost every successful interpretation of dreams. Details that may be lost soon after waking should be written while still fresh.

- Remember to give yourself grace on this journey. I, like you, have been frustrated after failing to write out the details of a dream, only to have them fade into forgotten space after I was fully awake.

This is not about perfection but about a journey to revelation. It's important to realize that, as with all great adventures, it starts with a single step. I pray this book allows you to accept the invitation from your Father to pay attention to your dreams. You don't have to accomplish everything in a single day. Maybe you can just start with a simple statement...

"Here I am, Lord. Speak for your servant is listening."

About The Authors

GEOERL NILES is the Senior Leader of The Calling Church in Vancouver, WA, along with his wife Julianne. Geoerl and Julianne also founded Ascend International Ministries, a Christian credentialing organization built around relationship and support of one another. He is passionate to see people come into a full understanding of their calling and purpose, and has traveled extensively to pursue that passion. Geoerl has been a Bethel Leaders Network leader since its beginning and loves the connection it brings. Geoerl has seven amazing children and six wonderful grandchildren! After all, building a legacy is a beautiful thing.

NANCY BOYD is the founder and president of Legacy House Ministries, a healing and equipping center in Central California. After serving as a Senior Pastor for over 20 years, Nancy is pursuing her deep passion to see Christians embrace their legacy for supernatural healing. She is a leader with Bethel Leaders Network, The River Revival Network, and a member of Shiloh Company. Nancy is the proud mother of four children and grandmother of seven. She is also a popular speaker, blogger and author of #God is STILL Good - #We

Are Still Winning and The Big Picture children's church curriculum Series - One through Four.

Made in the USA
Columbia, SC
24 January 2023

10102828R00052